THROUGH THE VALLEY

Through the Valley
The Way of the Cross for the End of Life

Susan Catherine Mitchell

Published 2009 by
Veritas Publications
7–8 Lower Abbey Street
Dublin 1
Ireland

Email publications@veritas.ie
Website www.veritas.ie

ISBN 978-1-84730-174-1

10 9 8 7 6 5 4 3 2 1

A catalogue record for this book is available from the British
Library.

Designed by Lir Mac Cárthaigh
Printed in Ireland by Hudson Killeen, Dublin

Veritas books are printed on paper made from the wood pulp of man-
aged forests. For every tree felled, at least one tree is planted, thereby
renewing natural resources.

For all those who accompany the dying, especially the staff and volunteers of Holy Cross Hospice in Silver Spring, Maryland, and Montgomery Hospice in Rockville, Maryland. You walk with God every day.

Preface

In April 2000, I received an urgent phone call at my home in Maryland; my father was dying. My family and I spent ten days with him in a Connecticut hospital. We journeyed together through the valley of the shadow of death (Psalm 23). At the time, I was finishing my studies at the Washington Theological Union, and one of my friends and mentors, Rev. Dominic Monti, OFM, told me that while before I had known the theology of Holy Week, now I knew its reality. My father, Anthony John Mitchell, died on Easter Sunday.

That experience led me to seek out training in the ministry of chaplaincy. Since then I have been a chaplain in a nursing facility for the elderly, a hospital, an inpatient hospice and in hospice patients' homes. I am board-certified by the National Association of Catholic Chaplains, which is sponsored by the US Conference of Catholic Bishops. I have listened to the stories of many journeys, been a witness to life and to death, to joy and to sorrow, to hope and to despair. The reflections in this book spring from these experiences. The end of life is a deeply holy and intense time. It can be a time for inner growth, for connection among people and connection to the Divine. It can also be painful, sad, exhausting and draining, all at the same time.

It is in this very intensity that we can break through to an awareness of the God who sustains us, a God who is both the very fiber of our being and so transcendent that we are stopped wordless in wonder. We do not come to God apart from our daily lives, but through them. What has given meaning and purpose to us throughout our lives is what will give meaning and purpose to us during our final days.

I envisioned this book of meditations as a way of immersing ourselves in the life of Jesus of Nazareth. The stops, or stations, along the way of the cross are not meant to be taken as strict analogies to our lives. The specific episodes in the life of Jesus are what he encountered as a perfect embodiment of our humanity, making manifest the Kingdom of God. While our specific episodes will be different, we walk in his way.

The point of connection is that our God became human and experienced the same pain, the same fear, the same anxiety and the same joy that we feel. This God is with us in all the times of our own lives. This God knows us, loves us and is never apart from us. The incarnation binds us ever more closely to the Divine and to each other. For we do not journey alone; we journey within a Trinity of Divine love and in the company of all creation. We live and move and have our being in an ever-connected universe. Our sufferings and our joys are joined inextricably together. It is in the creative and life-giving Spirit of God that we come together to reflect on the life of Jesus and on our own lives. I offer these meditations as a way of acknowledging our shared path. It is my hope that they will bring closeness and peace. Blessings on the journey!

Acknowledgements

I wish to thank those who reviewed an earlier version of this book, including Dr Megan McKenna, Sr Nelda Chafitelli, osu, Cynthia Chappell, Fr Joseph Wimmer, osa, and, of course, my husband, Art Fraas, and children, Mitchell and Catherine Fraas, for all their love and support. Any errors or omissions are, of course, my own.

Contents

Introduction

The way of the cross, or the stations of the cross, is a traditional liturgical service that allows those who cannot go to Jerusalem to figuratively walk on the path that Jesus walked. Most Roman Catholic churches have some kind of representation of these stations, usually on their walls. These traditional meditations combine Scripture with revered stories, such as those of Veronica and her veil. For this book, I have used the Scriptural Stations of the Cross set forth by Pope John Paul ii in 1991 as a way to be more faithful to the biblical narrative and to make them more appropriate for ecumenical purposes. I have used the texts suggested by the us Conference of Catholic Bishops on their website (www.usccb.org). To them I have added the Resurrection narrative of Luke. Other translations or appropriate readings could be used based on local needs.

This book is designed to be used both for personal reflection and as a liturgical service. The purpose of the liturgical service is to gather the dying and those who are caring for them on the way of the cross that Jesus followed, in the belief that we are all connected to a larger reality of pain and of hope.

The congregation will most likely include a larger number of family members and caregivers than those who are ill. I envision, for example, an inpatient hospice with grounds around it, such as one in which I have worked called Casey House, operated by Montgomery Hospice in Rockville, Maryland. I have written this liturgy with that setting in mind. Their hospice rooms have large windows overlooking a garden, with benches, a small pond and a walkway with memorial stones and trees. The beds can even be moved outdoors by family members.

The service could also be adapted for other settings, such as a church, hospital chapel, or an individual home. A group could perhaps even drive from place to place with each residence or facility representing a different station. Another approach would be to focus on one or two stations a week in a small prayer group or in individual reflection.

This is an ecumenical Christian service open to all. It can be seen as a walking meditation, a pilgrimage, a way to make manifest that we all walk together. It tells a universal story. With that in mind, it is important to honour the sensibilities of those who would be upset or offended to have it taking place outside their windows. Families of the dying have enough to contend with; they do not need to be reminded by the way of the cross of past injustices and pain inflicted in the name of Christianity.

While this service uses all of the stations, including the Resurrection, in practice it is important to consider individual needs and plan accordingly. For those in frail health, selecting a few stations would be more beneficial than having a long service. The hope of the Resurrection should always be included. When we reflect on the way of the cross, we are always looking back from the perspective of the Resurrection. The scripture writers gathered oral traditions and interpretations of eyewitnesses to compile the Good News. While we can focus on one part of Jesus' life and death, we can never forget the context of the gift of Resurrection open to all of us. Those who are suffering or in sorrow particularly need to hear its message, no matter how limited the time.

It is a good idea to provide copies of the scriptures ahead of time to encourage personal and family reflection. Distant friends and family members could also participate on their own at the same time. Use technology such as the internet or a mobile phone to connect them. Staff members and volunteers could be invited to participate, both to assist and for their own benefit.

If at all possible, the dying, their families, loved ones and caregivers should be asked ahead of time to give some of the brief reflections, in place of those written here, which are meant only as a starting point. My reflections may also need to be shortened to suit the needs of the congregation. That way, the service will better reflect the experience of the particular community and their fears and hopes. The presider or leader could then tie these reflections together and connect them to the larger reality. Participants should be selected to read the Scriptures aloud.

Traditionally, a cross is carried in procession during the stations. This could be done by one person, or families could each carry a cross. Pictures could be attached to each cross. Be creative! An intravenous pole or stand could also be used as a cross, since it serves as a stark symbol of death and debility to many, yet also carries the hope of relief. If there are children involved, they could draw or paint their rendition of the cross and carry it with them. Anything that draws the pain and suffering out of the person by some medium can be used here. That pain then becomes shared with the larger community of the dying. I have included suggestions of hymns, but again music that reflects the participants should be substituted whenever possible.

At the end of the service, have a living thing for the participants to take with them – a flower, a plant, a packet of seeds – that can act as a symbol of Resurrection hope. We want to connect our sufferings with those of Jesus and with the wider world, as it was in the beginning, is now and ever shall be. Along the way, we will acknowledge and connect our suffering, and it will be transformed into Easter joy and new life.

The arms of the Cross become the arms of God.
It is good. So, let us go.
Let us follow Jesus to the cross and death and
Resurrection.
Let us go with God.[1]

---

1. Megan McKenna, *The New Stations of the Cross*, xvi.

The First Station

Jesus prays in the garden of Gethsemane

SETTING
The Hospice Garden

HYMN SUGGESTION
Be not Afraid

LET US PRAY
We adore you O Christ, and we bless you, because by your holy cross and Resurrection you have redeemed the world.

READER
Then Jesus came with them to a place called Gethsemane, and he said to his disciples, 'Sit here while I go over there and pray.' He took along Peter and the two sons of Zebedee, and began to feel sorrow and distress. Then he said to them, 'My soul is sorrowful even to death.

Remain here and keep watch with me.' He advanced a little and fell prostrate in prayer, saying, 'My Father, if it is possible, let this cup pass from me; yet, not as I will, but as you will.' When he returned to his disciples he found them asleep. He said to Peter, 'So you could not keep watch with me for one hour? Watch and pray that you may not undergo the test. The spirit is willing, but the flesh is weak.' (Matthew 26:36-41)

Before any of us came to this place, we prayed that we would not have to be here. We prayed that the tests would come back negative, that the scans would show nothing, that we would laugh at our fears of the looming shadow. Well, we are here, in this place, this garden, and we are still praying. Some of us are praying for bodily healing, and that is all right. Some of us are praying for a healing of mind and spirit, for the strength to go on, and that is all right. Some of us do not know for what we are praying, and that is all right too.

For Jesus too prayed in the garden. He took himself away, hoping that his disciples would watch with him. He asked his heavenly Father to take the cup from him if that was God's will, but affirmed that he would be faithful no matter what. Jesus placed himself inside the healing power of God and trusted. He trusted that no matter what happened, God would be with him. This passage shows Jesus' humanity to the fullest, and it echoes a prayer that many of us have made: if only … if only …

Perhaps we are in the position of the disciples. We are trying to be faithful, to watch with someone we love who is in agony, but we are weary to the bone. We need to sleep. It does not matter, for we are all in the garden together. We each have our private fears and anxieties that we voice to God deep in our hearts. No prayer is unworthy, no petition too small or too large. We are all in the garden together. Some of us can sleep while others watch. Sometimes we are surprised at who is in the garden with us. People we barely know are supporting us, rising to the occasion, while others cannot even go this far.

Dear God, we come before you in this splendid garden of your earth. We are your people, and we pray to you to go before us on this journey of ours. We pray in solidarity with all those who suffer, whether from illness or despair, loneliness or poverty or war. We honour you and give thanks for all the many blessings of this bountiful earth, which has nourished us all of our lives. We go forth in hope, travelling together.

Begin walking around the paths or by a predetermined route. Walk in silence or have instrumental music playing softly.

The Second Station

Jesus, betrayed by Judas, is arrested

LET US PRAY

We adore you O Christ, and we bless you, because by your holy cross and Resurrection you have redeemed the world.

READER

Then, while Jesus was still speaking, Judas, one of the Twelve, arrived, accompanied by a crowd with swords and clubs, who had come from the chief priests, the scribes, and the elders. His betrayer had arranged a signal with them, saying, 'The man I shall kiss is the one; arrest him and lead him away securely.' He came and immediately went over to him and said, 'Rabbi'. And he kissed him. At this they laid hands on him and arrested him. (Mark 14:43-46)

The name of Judas has entered into popular culture and language to mean one who betrays another. The betrayer is someone close, a friend whom we trusted but who has now turned on us. When we are ill or dying, many of us feel that we have been betrayed by our own bodies. These bodies that have kept us going throughout the years suddenly won't cooperate anymore. We feel betrayed. Why has this happened? Haven't we treated our bodies well? Taken care of them?

Perhaps we feel betrayed by a loved one, a grown child who is not with us, a friend who does not care. We feel blindsided – this blow we did not expect. Judas, of course, felt great remorse at his act and ended his own life. While we do not want to take this analogy too far, it is important to remember that we do not know what is going on in another person's life. Our families and friends may have illnesses, problems or concerns of their own that we do not know about. They may simply be unable to cope. Our own bodies may have just had enough. There is nothing we can do about it now.

Dear God, help us to acknowledge the weaknesses of others and of ourselves. Help us to accept our own failings and to understand those of others. You are the one who will never betray us, never fail us. Help us to put our trust in you.

The Third Station

Jesus is condemned by the Sanhedrin

❦

We adore you O Christ, and we bless you, because by your holy cross and Resurrection you have redeemed the world.

READER
When day came the council of elders of the people met, both chief priests and scribes, and they brought him before their Sanhedrin. They said, 'If you are the Messiah, tell us.' But he replied to them, 'If I tell you, you will not believe, and if I question, you will not respond. But from this time on the Son of Man will be seated at the right hand of the power of God.' They all asked, 'Are you then the Son of God?' He replied to them, 'You say that I am.' Then they said, 'What further need have we for testimony? We have heard it from his own mouth.' (Luke 22:66-71)

Jesus lived his whole life in such a way as to bring about the Kingdom of God. He spoke to small groups and to large ones. He healed the sick and preached of love and compassion and redemption. Still the religious authorities and those in power did not understand.

We too have heard God's message throughout our lives, and we too do not understand. At the end of life, some people begin to question their entire belief system. They wonder what they have missed. Some people feel that if they have believed in God and have lived a good life, they should not suffer or die. Others who have not believed begin to wonder.

We have no more need of testimony at this time, but rather of presence. Whether we are dying, or accompanying the dying, it is time for us to ponder the presence of God in our lives and how we have responded. God has spoken to us in many ways: through the love we have given and received, through the splendour of nature and of science, through the Scriptures and the Sacraments, through our own reason and our ability to tell right from wrong, through the actions of others and through our own journey so far.

Sometimes people who are dying want to know what else they can do at this time. My answer is to stop doing and start being – be aware and open to God. I encourage people to lie back in the embrace of a God who loves them and cares for them. It is God who is directing our journey. We need only be open to listen and to receive. We know more than we think we know; we just need to believe it and live in God's love.

Dear God, help us to open our hearts and minds and souls to you. Help us to appreciate all you have done in our lives. Help us to stop trying to analyse you and to start loving and receiving you.

The Fourth Station

Jesus is denied by Peter

LET US PRAY

*We adore you O Christ, and we bless you,
because by your holy cross and Resurrection you
have redeemed the world.*

READER

*Now Peter was sitting outside in the courtyard.
One of the maids came over to him, and said,
'You too were with Jesus the Galilean.' But he
denied it in front of everyone, saying, 'I do not
know what you are talking about!' As he went
out to the gate, another girl saw him, and said
to those who were there. 'This man was with
Jesus the Nazarean.' Again, he denied it with an
oath, 'I do not know the man!' A little later the
bystanders came over and said to Peter, 'Surely
you too are one of them; even your speech gives
you away.' At that he began to curse and to*

swear, 'I do not know the man.' And immediately a cock crowed. Then Peter remembered the words that Jesus had spoken: 'Before the cock crows you will deny me three times.' He went out and began to weep bitterly. (Matthew 26:69-75)

In the gospels, Peter stands out as one who takes a long time to understand things. He makes mistakes and is befuddled by the mystery of Jesus. He is a mirror to our own insecurities and doubts. Here Peter is frightened. Jesus has been taken away by the authorities and may be executed. Peter, as a follower of his, may be next. Peter is faithful enough to stay close, but is fearful of being caught hanging around. He reacts instinctively to deny Jesus and his own association with him. He wants to protect himself.

We often react in the same way. When we are ill, we deny that much is going on. We think, 'It is only a small lump', or, 'I have a good doctor'. We cling to denial with our loved ones: 'She is too young, this can't be happening', or, 'He has come through so much before, he can't be dying now'. In an odd way, when a person has lived a long, healthy life, we unconsciously think that he or she will never die. For example, we simply cannot imagine our elderly parents not being in our lives.

We do not want to talk about debility with the ageing or death with the dying. We say it is because we do not want to upset them, but isn't it as much not to upset ourselves? If we do not talk about it, we can pretend it is not happening. We deny our own ageing, and death remains a taboo subject.

Sometimes people who deny the reality of death believe they are acting out of hope that God will intervene, that somehow it is a lack of faith to talk about death. However, talking about death does not mean that God cannot cure our loved ones. It is not lack of faith in God to accept death; rather, it is an affirmation of God's life-giving power that while our earthly lives will come to an end, God's love will continue. We will be with God and our loved ones in a more intense way.

I have known many families who could talk freely about the dying process, bless each other and say goodbye. It is difficult, yes, but it is so liberating to say the words out loud, to share the journey together and not to be afraid. We give our loved ones a great gift if we can do this at some level.

Finally, we should remember that the Risen Christ forgave Peter his denial and made him the leader of the disciples. We need to be gentle with those who cannot accept the reality of death and not try to press on them some sort of an 'ideal death'. Perhaps we can nudge them along gently, assuage their fears and help them to come to a deeper understanding of God's love in their own way. For God is with them on their journey, even if they cannot accept that they are even on the road.

Dear God, help us to be open to the intertwined realities of life and death. Help us to live deliberately and openly in your presence, trusting that you are leading us in your way.

The Fifth Station

Jesus is judged by Pilate

LET US PRAY

We adore you O Christ, and we bless you, because by your holy cross and Resurrection you have redeemed the world.

READER

The chief priests with the elders and the scribes, that is, the whole Sanhedrin, held a council. They bound Jesus, led him away, and handed him over to Pilate. Pilate questioned him, 'Are you the king of the Jews?' He said to him in reply, 'You say so.' The chief priests accused him of many things. Again Pilate questioned him, 'Have you no answer? See how many things they accuse you of.' Jesus gave him no further answer, so that Pilate was amazed ... Pilate, wishing to satisfy the crowd, released Barabbas and handed Jesus over to be crucified. (Mark 15:1-5, 15)

What is this man guilty of? Jesus, the one without sin, has been condemned to death by crucifixion. The authorities, the experts, have decided he will die. When we first heard that our loved one was going to die, that curative medicine could do no more, it may have felt like a death sentence. People react in many ways to the news that they are going to die. Some feel anger at the medical establishment, others feel guilt that they didn't take care of themselves, and others still feel relief that the words have finally been said. Some fear the dying process, how it will happen and separation from those they love.

Spiritual distress can occur when we feel, 'This isn't the way it was supposed to be'. We may have had an image in our minds and in our hearts of our later years, and this was not it. We may feel that we have lived a good life, done all the right things, and still God is letting us down, letting us die. We may feel judged by our sins and found wanting. We may just feel exhausted and unable to let it sink in.

There may be a period of intense activity, making arrangements, contacting friends and being busy. Then a quiet time can set in when the journey really begins. We are here, we are supported by those who love us and we are on holy ground. We do not know what to expect, but the preliminaries are over. We must begin.

Dear God, we are reeling from the news that our lives have changed. Help us as we set out on uncharted ground. Be with us and our families and with those who care for us in so many ways. Be with those who have no one to be with them, those who have no care. Extend our compassion to all those who suffer, and our trust that you are with all of us.

The Sixth Station

Jesus is scourged and crowned with thorns

❦

LET US PRAY
We adore you O Christ, and we bless you,
because by your holy cross and Resurrection you
have redeemed the world.

READER
Then Pilate took Jesus and had him scourged.
And the soldiers wove a crown out of thorns
and placed it on his head, and clothed him in a
purple cloak, and they came to him and said,
'Hail, King of the Jews!' And they struck him
repeatedly. (John 19:1-3)

❦

Now we come to the pain: throbbing, pounding, burning, itching, stabbing, numbing, exhausting pain. In the image of Jesus crowned with thorns we enter into our own pain and the pain of those of whom we accompany on this journey. We have endured stabs of pain, waves of pain, nausea, constipation, diarrhoea, vomiting, vertigo and breathlessness. We have felt helpless and lost, unable even to scream. Some days we do scream: we rail, we cry, we throw things and we damn God and all those around us. Other days we endure: we stay quiet and hope the pain will not notice us, that it will go away if we do not pay attention. Some days we are able to escape the pain, to sleep, to have it lifted by drugs or meditation, or music, or children, or being able to eat again for the first time.

Sometimes we inadvertently increase our pain by needless guilt, recriminations, such as: why didn't I stop smoking, eat better, break off an abusive relationship? At this point, it does not really matter. The pain has taken on a life of its own. We need to do whatever we can to get through it, to continue our journey, to relate to others and to God.

We can find release and hope in the idea of redemptive suffering. In its purest form, it acknowledges that some pain cannot be completely relieved and must be endured. We offer our sufferings for the remission of sins – our own sins and those of others. We offer our very lives, as Jesus did. We reach out in compassion to all those who suffer. We let go of our sufferings and become united to a universal whole. We can imagine ourselves as individual drops in an ocean of healing water, or as pure energy coursing through the cosmos.

Or, more traditionally, we can feel ourselves dwelling within the all-encompassing Sacred Heart of Jesus, radiating love to the world. Meditating on this kind of union can make us more aware of the divine being that suffuses us with life.

However, redemptive suffering is a dangerous concept. Pain for the sake of pain does not help anyone. We must be very careful here. God does not want or will us to suffer! If the pain can be relieved or palliated in a way that allows us to function, holding on to it as a matter of pride or principle could lead to idolising the pain itself.

We must remember that we are not being punished for our sins by our illness or death. We are reaping the consequences of the imperfections of our human body, will and mind, and of our very limited lifespan. Our God is a God of mercy. Jesus healed in mind and body with the fullness of the Holy Spirit. We need to ask for this healing, for this spirit of life amidst the pain of death. We also need to be aware of and to accept that healing when it comes in the form of medications, or other palliative measures of the body and soul. We have become an empty vessel, poured out as Jesus was, empty of our guilt and our preconceptions. We receive the love of God and the peace that passes all understanding.

Dear God, we pray for you to be with us in our suffering, as we receive a crown of thorns and blows to our body and soul. Help us to endure with the help of others. Help us to join our sufferings to you and to those who suffer on this earth. We thank you for all those who are with us at this time, for medical researchers, pharmacists and doctors, and all healthcare and spiritual care providers, for all who bring comfort and hope to us. We thank you for our families, our friends and all who show us that we are never alone, that you are always with us.

The Seventh Station

Jesus bears his cross

LET US PRAY

We adore you O Christ, and we bless you, because by your holy cross and Resurrection you have redeemed the world.

READER

When the chief priests and the guards saw Jesus they cried out, 'Crucify him, crucify him!' Pilate said to them, 'Take him yourselves and crucify him. I find no guilt in him.' … They cried out, 'Take him away, take him away! Crucify him!' Pilate said to them, 'Shall I crucify your king?' The chief priests answered, 'We have no king but Caesar.' Then he handed him over to them to be crucified. So they took Jesus, and carrying the cross himself he went out to what is called the Place of the Skull, in Hebrew, Golgotha. (John 19:6, 15-17)

Jesus takes up his cross and begins to walk. It is large and heavy and he has a distance to go, through the city and up the hill. The cross was a symbol of shame in the world in which Jesus lived. It was a sign of disgrace, of failure, of suppression by the Roman authorities. In our youth-obsessed culture, illness and death are sometimes seen as failure. People are much more willing to talk about sex than death.

Looking at the cross from a broader perspective, it is a disgrace that in our modern world, millions are without food and shelter and medical care, and succumb to illness and pain that could have been prevented. We should not pretty-up the cross. 'The poor carry the cross all the time, and Jesus carries all the poor'.[2]

Jesus is also carrying us. Jesus knows our burdens because he is bearing them as well. When we feel the weight of sorrow, or pain, or fear or uncertainty, we know Jesus is yoked to us and that our burden is lightened. This does not mean we should seek out pain or crosses to bear – there is enough suffering in the world. As we walk with Jesus, we are grateful for the lives that we have lived, through all the ups and downs. This is a good station in which to consider our entire lives, our entire journey from God to God. We live and move and have our being in God. Nothing is apart from that – no sorrow, no joy. We are connected to the Divine through

---

1. Megan McKenna, *The New Stations of the Cross*, p. 53.

the outstretched arms of each other within the love of the Trinity, manifest in the Holy Spirit. The cross is a powerful symbol of that unity and that belonging.

Dear God, we place ourselves in you. We feel your presence always in the presence of all your people. Help us to learn how to carry our crosses and to let go of the burdens that are not ours. We thank you for being with us and carrying us along the way.

The Eighth Station

Jesus is helped by Simon the Cyrene

🍃

LET US PRAY
*We adore you O Christ, and we bless you,
because by your holy cross and Resurrection you
have redeemed the world.*

READER
*They pressed into service a passerby, Simon, a
Cyrenian, who was coming in from the
country, the father of Alexander and Rufus, to
carry his cross.* (Mark 15:21)

🍃

We do not carry the cross alone. Some are pressed into
service to help us, some come willingly forward. Often
those who are ill will protest that they do not want to be
a burden to their families or others. We are a very inde-
pendent society – and sometimes a lonely one. Depend-

ency is seen as a problem, a weakness, but we are all interdependent on each other. Even before the time of our dying, we rely on others. We rely on our immediate family and on social institutions to raise us when we are young. We rely on educators, on healthcare professionals, on farm labourers, on sanitation workers and on those who govern us and protect us. We rely not just on our own community, but in this increasingly global world, on others whose existence we do not even acknowledge.

So in our time of dying, it is only natural that we rely on those closest to us, and on those who have answered the call to work with others. We need not be ashamed to ask for help, for relief, for forgiveness, for release. Jesus accepted Simon. Who have we helped in our lives? Whose crosses have we helped to bear? When have we been Simon?

Dear God, we acknowledge your presence in all those who help us along the way, and in all whom we help. Help us to appreciate all who have been with us along the way. Help us to hear your call to be open, both to giving and to receiving.

The Ninth Station

Jesus meets the women of Jerusalem

LET US PRAY
We adore you O Christ, and we bless you,
because by your holy cross and Resurrection you
have redeemed the world.

READER
A large crowd of people followed Jesus, including
many women who mourned and lamented him.
Jesus turned to them and said, 'Daughters of
Jerusalem, do not weep for me; weep instead for
yourselves and for your children, for indeed, the
days are coming when people will say, "Blessed
are the barren, the wombs that never bore and
the breasts that never nursed." At that time,
people will say to the mountains, "Fall upon us"
and to the hills, "cover us!" for if these things are
done when the wood is green what will happen
when it is dry?' (Luke 23:27-31)

The traditional interpretation of this passage is that it refers to the upcoming fall of Jerusalem. Jesus is saying that those without children will be glad that they did not live to see them suffer. These are harsh words indeed.

The loss of an infant or a child brings a sharp stinging kind of sorrow. When parents lose a baby, their grief is sometimes hidden from the world. Parents often do not know how to share this grief, who to tell, or what to do. Friends and family members do not know what to say, and casual acquaintances often wound with careless comments, such as, 'You are young, you can have another', or 'It's better/easier/less painful this way than if the child was older', or, even worse, 'It is God's will', or, 'God needed another angel in heaven'.

Parents whose child is seriously ill inhabit a world apart. All their attention is focused on that small person. They yearn to hold their child, to will him or her to health and life. Even after death or stillbirth, this physical closeness brings a kind of fierce joy and sorrow mingled together. Parents often need rituals of blessing and mourning, of acknowledgment that their child is real and beloved of God.

In this station, Jesus is speaking to all those who mourn their children, who are lost from many causes, whether they be children or adults in a harsh world. Jesus is asking us to share our mourning for our own losses with the losses of all. When a child dies before a mother or father, there is a deep sense of wrongness and spiritual distress. Many parents find solace in sharing their feelings and experiences with others. They often also rally for better healthcare and treatment, to provide hope for those who have very little.

When an older child is dying, he or she is often very aware of it and will actually help the parents to cope. It can be a relief for the child to be able to speak about the process, and to be a child for a little longer.

This station speaks to all our fears of loss of childhood innocence as well. Parents want to be able to protect their children, but they cannot. Jesus is calling upon us to be with all the children of the world and to extend our compassion to them and to their families.

Dear God, Divine Mother, we are all your children. Help us to be with each other in our grief and to reach out to your loving care. Help us to trust that you are cradling us in your loving arms as we continue along on our way. Help us to grow into your love, as a child grows to become an adult.

The Tenth Station

Jesus is crucified

✿

LET US PRAY
We adore you O Christ, and we bless you, because by your holy cross and Resurrection you have redeemed the world.

READER
When they came to the place called the skull, they crucified him and the criminals there, one on his right, the other on his left. Then Jesus said, 'Father, forgive them they know not what they do'. (Luke: 23:33-34)

✿

How many times can it be said of us that we know not what we do? We blunder along in our lives, thinking we know best but often miss out on what is important. Many times a dying person or his or her loved ones will wish that they had known death was coming. Then they would have done the things they had always planned to do, gone places and seen people they had always meant to see. Regret is a powerful emotion. We do not want to admit that we are all mortal, that we will also die someday. We live our lives unaware of what is truly significant and important, until some event, such as a death, shocks us awake.

We do not see Jesus right in front of us being crucified on a cross of poverty, war, disease and deprivation. We do not see Jesus in our families or in our neighbours who need our help. We do not see Jesus in ourselves, as we become convinced that we are worthless and nothing will ever change in our lives. What do we need to shock us out of our complacency into compassion and under-standing? Who needs to be crucified?

Jesus forgave those who acted unthinkingly, unknow-ingly and who nailed him to a cross. Do we forgive easily? If we are aware of another's real shortcomings and they do not want to listen to us, do we forgive them? Do we say, 'I told you so' when our prescience is proved correct? When a loved one unthinkingly hurts us, do we hold a grudge? Some people can trace all of the wrong-doings inflicted upon them throughout their lives. Holding on to bad times can poison us from within.

Dear God, help us to be aware of ourselves and our lives and our very blessedness in the eyes of God. Let us live each day aware that time is precious and that this day will never come again. Help us to forgive those who have injured us, and to reach out to those whom we have injured. Help us to let go of poisonous resentments and to live freely this day and every day of our lives.

The Eleventh Station

Jesus promises his kingdom to the good thief

❧

LET US PRAY
We adore you O Christ, and we bless you, because by your holy cross and Resurrection you have redeemed the world.

READER
Now one of the criminals hanging there reviled Jesus, saying, 'Are you not the Messiah? Save yourself and us.' The other, however, rebuking him, said in reply, 'Have you no fear of God, for you are subject to the same condemnation? And indeed, we have been condemned justly, for the sentence we received corresponds to our crimes, but this man has done nothing criminal.' Then he said, 'Jesus remember me when you come into your kingdom.' He replied to him, 'Amen I say to you, today you will be with me in Paradise.'
(Luke 23:39-43)

Sometimes people say that we die as we live. This was true for Jesus and for the unrepentant thief. Jesus died the way he lived, preaching the gospel of God's kingdom on earth, which included forgiveness and mercy. The thief who condemned him died as a consequence of his crimes, reviling the one who could have saved him. The good thief, however, acknowledged that he was guilty and deserved punishment, but asked Jesus to remember him. He took the chance of being condemned further; he trusted in the one hanging next to him. He reached for grace, for God, at the moment of his death.

Jesus in turn did not hesitate to forgive him his very real sins. Jesus did not want to know all the details or to weigh the pros and cons. He simply said to him, 'Today, this day, you will be with me in Paradise'.

Sometimes we do not believe that we are worthy of forgiveness. We focus on sins of the past that have long been forgiven, not believing that we are indeed free of them. Some of us do not want to ask for forgiveness for heinous sins that we think no one could forgive. We hold on to our guilt and it pollutes us and all those around us. We fear death for we believe we will be punished. We think our sins are greater than God. We do not want to let go of our sins. We do not believe that today, this day, we are forgiven, and that we are living in the paradise which God has created for us. We waste the chance for grace, we do not ask those around us or our God for forgiveness and mercy.

Jesus does not follow the rules. He reaches through them and beyond them to the human heart and soul. He challenges us from the cross to reach out to others who ask for our help and our forgiveness, for whom this earth is not the paradise that God intended.

Dear God, help us to acknowledge that we need to be forgiven. Help us to let go of both our sins and our guilt. Help us to believe that today, this very day, that we live and breathe and dwell in your presence. Help us to believe that when we pray the Lord's prayer we are called to enter into your kingdom on earth as it is in heaven. Help us to build your kingdom here on earth, and to forgive as you forgive. At the moment of our death, help us to reach for your love and forgiveness.

The Twelfth Station

Jesus speaks to his mother and the Disciples

LET US PRAY

We adore you O Christ, and we bless you, because by your holy cross and Resurrection you have redeemed the world.

READER

Standing by the cross of Jesus were his mother and his mother's sister, Mary, the wife of Cleopas, and Mary of Magdala. When Jesus saw his mother and the disciple there whom he loved, he said to his mother, 'Woman, behold, your son'. Then he said to the disciple, 'Behold, your mother'. And from that hour the disciple took her into his home. (John 19:25-27)

Here we see Jesus taking care of things from the cross. He ensures that his mother, Mary, will be provided for after his death. Mothers and fathers alike often try to prepare their families for their own deaths. Like Jesus, they try to anticipate what will happen when they are gone and provide for those who will need help. I once worked with a young mother who planned her four children's birthday parties before she died. Often people tell me that they are not afraid for themselves, but for those they are leaving behind. They work out financial arrangements or plan their own memorial services. They take care of things.

We too need to think of our end times. What do we need to say from the cross? Who has taken care of us, mothered us through our life? Who do we need to care for?

In addition, Jesus' mother is revered in many cultures. In Ephesus, Turkey, where by tradition John brought Mary to live, there is a tiny church built above the remains of an early Christian settlement. In that church, Mary is honoured by inscriptions from many faiths, including Islam. In Catholic tradition, Mary becomes the mother of all through this statement of Jesus from the cross. We are all encouraged to pray through Mary to Jesus. We have a heavenly mother to turn to, even if our earthly mother has gone.

This is a good station in which to think about our own beloved dead. What are our own personal beliefs about the afterlife? What do we think will happen to us? In the Catholic interpretation of the communion of saints, we believe that we can pray for the souls of the departed and help them on their way to fullness with God. As well, we believe that those souls who are with God can pray for our well-being and our souls. Our connections to the living do not end with death.

Dear God, help us to say goodbye to our loved ones, to prepare them for what is to come. Help us to remember those who have died and to connect with them, with Mary and with all the communion of saints.

The Thirteenth Station

Jesus dies on the cross

Hymn suggestion
Were You There When They Crucified My Lord?

Let us pray
We adore you O Christ, and we bless you, because by your holy cross and Resurrection you have redeemed the world.

Reader
It was now about noon and darkness came over the whole land until three in the afternoon because of an eclipse of the sun. Then the veil of temple was torn down the middle. Jesus cried out in a loud voice, 'Father, into your hands I commend my spirit'; and then when he had said this he breathed his last. (Luke 23:44-46)

So here we are at death. We do not know what it feels like to die. Even if we have watched others take their last breaths and dissolve into silence, we do not know how we ourselves will die.

The unknown, the unthinkable has happened; our world has been torn apart. We have climbed the hill and finished the journey. Perhaps it has seemed long and agonising and we are relieved, or perhaps it has come too soon. There is often surprise at death – that it actually happens. It has been accomplished, and while grief tears at our hearts, we feel a calm connection that extends beyond the moment.

We take this time to pause, to take our bearings, to be quiet and to enter into the stillness of eternity. Our ordinary fears have been driven out and have died as well. Our only remaining fear is the deep reverence called fear of the Lord. We are stunned at the power of God, at the mystery of life, which is fully revealed only when life is gone, when the body is empty. We are profoundly grateful that our loved one is suffering no more and is with God. We commend our own spirits to the Divine One and rest awhile in God's embrace. Let us take some time in silence to remember all those who have left this life for another. Let us just be.

Pause for two minutes in silence. Then walk back in silence about half way to the beginning point.

The Fourteenth Station

Jesus is placed in the tomb

LET US PRAY
We adore you O Christ, and we bless you, because by your holy cross and Resurrection you have redeemed the world.

READER
When it was evening, there came a rich man from Arimathea named Joseph, who was himself a disciple of Jesus. He went to Pilate and asked for the body of Jesus; then Pilate ordered it to be handed over. Taking the body, Joseph wrapped it in clean linen and laid it in his new tomb that he had hewn in the rock. Then he rolled a huge stone across the entrance to the tomb and departed. (Matthew 27:57-60)

Now there are things to do. A wake, a funeral, a memorial service, people to call, notices to write – a whole host of activities. Some people throw themselves into action, being efficient, taking care of others. They are the ones who always seem to know what to do. They will grieve later and may need help then. Others seem almost paralysed and cannot move. They need to be taken care of now. Both are forms of grieving and both need to be honoured as such.

Life as we have always known it has ended. There are tears, arguments and recriminations, laughter and remembrances, family reunions or family absences, sleepless nights or a deep sleep at last. We are in the between time – between our previous life and our new life, whatever that may turn out to be. We are lost in new territory. The poet Donald Hall wrote after his wife's death:

> When I try talking with strangers
> I want to run out of the room
> into the woods with turkeys and foxes.
> I want to talk only
> about words we spoke back and forth
> when we knew you would die.
> I want never to joke or argue
> or chatter again. I want never
> to think or feel.[3]

---

3. Donald Hall, excerpt from 'Letter at Christmas', *Without*, p. 63.

Dear God, help us in our between time. Help us to stay here for a while and just be. Help us as we go back and forth from our remembrance of the past to the terrors of the future. Help us to do whatever we need to do at this time and to let go of any expectations we or others hold of us. Be with us, as we need you to be.

Walk back in silence to the beginning point.

The Fifteenth Station

Jesus rises from the dead

♦

SETTING
Back in the garden where the stations started.

LET US PRAY
We adore you O Christ, and we bless you, because by your holy cross and Resurrection you have redeemed the world.

READER
On the first day of the week at dawn, the women came to the tomb bringing the spices they had prepared. They found the stone rolled back from the tomb; but when they entered the tomb, they did not find the body of the Lord Jesus. While they were still at a loss over what to think of this, two men in dazzling garments stood beside them. Terrified, the women bowed to the ground. The men said to them: 'Why do

you search for the Living One among the dead?
He is not here; he has been raised up.'
(Luke 24:1-5a)

The women did not find the body – they were looking for the Living One among the dead. Jesus has been raised up. He is risen. We are back in the garden, but it has been transformed. The tomb of the earth has given birth to new life. The fear of death has been exploded into the joy of resurrection. We have been changed by our journey and are no longer at a loss of what to think. We have travelled the way of the Cross and we have reached resurrection.

> No longer having to hate, no longer needing to
> be afraid, being able to affirm the great Yes
> that faith signifies, all this includes our learning
> to die.
> By living freer from fear, we will learn to
> die freer from fear. The more we become a part of
> the love with which we know we are united, the
> more immortal we are. Speaking in Christian
> terms, death is always behind us, but love is before
> us.[4]

---

4. Dorothee Soelle, *The Mystery of Death*, p. 128.

LET US PRAY

Let us take this love, this freedom from fear, this resurrection moment, and go out into a world which desperately needs to hear the Good News. We are beginning a new journey, one of hope and of understanding. Let us rejoice, for he is risen – for we have all died in Christ and now we will live in him. Let us go and live in the peace of Christ, alleluia, alleluia. Thanks be to God, alleluia, alleluia.

Instrumental music of an Easter Hymn. Participants should receive a flower, a bulb or some other symbol of hope as they leave the worship space.

Resources

Hall, Donald, *Without*, New York: Houghton Mifflin Harcourt, 1999.

McKenna, Megan, *The New Stations of the Cross*, New York: Doubleday, 2003.

Soelle, Dorothee, translated by Nancy Lukens-Rumscheidt, *The Mystery of Death*, Minneapolis: Fortress Press, 2007.